THE
FORCE
OF
FAVOR

D A V E   M A R T I N

Unless otherwise indicated, all Scripture quotations are taken from the New International Version of the Bible.

The Force of Favor
ISBN 0-9700987-0-7
Copyright ©2000 by Dave Martin

Published by Favor International
P.O. Box 608150 Orlando, FL 32860
Printed in the United States of America. All rights reserved under International Copyright law. Contents and/or cover may not be reproduced in whole or in part in any form without the express written consent of the Publisher.

FOREWORD

When God Sees A Problem, He Anoints A Man To Solve It. That is why I consider this book by Dave Martin so valuable.

Favor is the master key to recovering everything satan has stolen from your life. Favor is the golden secret to smashing the locks on the prison of debt. It is the major bridge from the common life to the uncommon life.

The Body of Christ needs this message. Ministers need this Wisdom.

I know the *Man.*
I believe his *Message.*
I have seen the *Mantle* on him.
The Anointing on him unlocks Favor...everywhere he goes.

How thankful I am that Dave Martin has invested the time to document these Master Secrets for us.

It is the most powerful Book on Favor that I have ever read.

— Mike Murdock

WHY I WROTE THIS BOOK

Over the past couple of years I have heard many sermons on the year of Jubilee. They were great and powerful messages about what God will do every 50 years during the year of Jubilee. I was so excited and ready to preach my own message on Jubilee when God said No.

I was so upset. I mean my heroes were preaching Jubilee. My friends were preaching Jubilee, and God said, "No, I have something else for you." I was reading a passage of scripture one day that is so familiar to all of us, and God showed me the message he wanted me to preach.

"The Spirit of the Sovereign Lord is on me, because the Lord has anointed me to preach good news to the poor. He has sent me to bind up the brokenhearted, to proclaim freedom for the captives and release for the prisoners, to proclaim the year of the Lord's Favor." (ISAIAH 61:1,2)

He said I want you to proclaim the year of the Lord's Favor. I said great, and which year is that. You know Jubilee is every 50 years, and I wasn't sure which year was the year of His Favor. He said every year is the year of my Favor.

I want you to go and teach people how to recognize, accept, and live in the Favor of God.

TABLE OF CONTENTS

CHAPTER

INTRODUCTION

I believe that Favor is the greatest harvest that you could ever receive from God.

Favor is better than money. Money cannot buy you Favor, but Favor can bring you money.

Favor will determine the level of your income.

Favor will show up in your life when you associate with the right people.

Favor will leave your life when you associate with the wrong people.

People are like elevators....they will take you up, or they will take you down. The people we spend our time with are so much more important to our future than we realize. If you want to be a success in life you need to get around people who have already been where you want to go.

Favor will cause you to regain in a day what Satan has stolen from you for years.

Stop and think for 30 seconds of the things that Satan has stolen from you, your family, and your business. Now see it all coming back to your house. Thank God for His Favor!

Favor can change a negative medical report.

We saw this happen when Sarah was barren in her womb. She could not produce a child, but the Bible says that God showed her Favor, and she brought forth a child.

You may have cancer in your body today, and it is totally gone tomorrow when God shows you Favor.

Favor is a seed that can be sown.

You have the ability to sow Favor into the lives of others and expect Favor to come back to you as a harvest. *"Do not be deceived: God cannot be mocked. A man reaps what he sows."* (GALATIANS 6:7)

The thing is…we can not give up if the harvest doesn't come tomorrow. I want to encourage you to keep sowing. Ask God to show you places to sow.

Christine and I try to sow something every day because we want to reap something every day. So we look for opportunities to sow. I encourage you to look for every opportunity you can find to sow Favor.

You may want to sow Favor into your pastor and his wife. You may sow Favor into your mentor. You can sow Favor to your spouse, your children, or even your parents.

"Let us not become weary in doing good, for at the proper time we will reap a harvest if we do not give up. Therefore, as we have opportunity, let us do good

**to all people, especially to those who belong
to the family of believers."** (GALATIANS 6:9-10)

"And Jesus grew in wisdom and stature, and in favor with God and men." (LUKE 2:52) We can see from this verse that it is possible to increase in Favor with God and man. That is why this book is so important to your life. It will teach you powerful principles for increasing in Favor.

I believe that this book will encourage you to begin to expect Favor to increase in your life, in your home, in your ministry, and in your business.

God has no limitations. So why have we limited him?

I want to encourage you in this book to take the limits off God. I am ready for Unlimited Favor. Favor that you can't even imagine. So much Favor that you can't keep track of everything that happens in a day.

I want to share with you the testimony of how Christine and I began to recognize, accept, and walk in the mantle of Favor that God has placed on our lives and ministry. I don't fully understand it, and can't fully explain it, but God has shown us the most incredible miracles of Favor. Now everywhere we go and everyone we come in contact with begins to experience an increase in understanding and an increase in Favor.

In December of 1997 we heard an incredible teaching by Dr. Mike Murdock from Deuteronomy 1:11 on the thousand times more blessing. It was incredible. It was powerful. And it was life changing.

"May the Lord, the God of your fathers, increase you a thousand times and bless you as he has promised!"

(DEUTERONOMY. 1:11)

We could not believe that we had missed this scripture for years. God would give us a thousand times more of anything we needed or wanted: joy, wisdom, health, peace, miracles, finances, love, anointing, power, victories, and FAVOR!

We could receive a thousand times more Favor than we have ever had.

I said to Christine, "We have to sow a seed for a thousand times more Favor to begin to flow in our life." She was in agreement, and we began to ask God what kind of seed to sow. The first thing I thought of was a $1,000 seed to represent a thousand times more. Well, we opened our check book to prepare the seed and found out we didn't have a $1,000. I was disappointed and asked God, "What can we do?"

Then God spoke to us to plant a $111 seed to represent Deuteronomy 1:11. I said, "We can do that." I actually planted one for me, one for Christine, and one for our ministry…a total of $333. In the pages of this book you will hear just a few of the testimonies that began to happen in our lives and the lives of others who have done the same. They began to experience the harvest of a thousand times more Favor.

It was less than two weeks after we had sown this $111 seed that a lady was visiting our house. She told us that the Holy Spirit had spoken to her and told her that she was to buy us something for our house. She asked what we need-ed, and I told her that there was this bed that we had been looking at for our bedroom. She said that she wanted to buy it for us.

Only a month later we received another incredible miracle of Favor. We had been praying for Christine's grandfather to give his heart to God. He was 74 years old, and the number of people over the age of 50 who surrender their lives to God is so small. We knew that we needed a miracle. Well, we got it! Grandpa Olsen lifted his hand to an altar call at Pastor Sherman Owens church in Sarasota, Florida while Dr. Mike Murdock was ministering there.

Praise the Lord for a thousand times more Favor!

I know you need increase. You have a God desire on the inside of you for increase. God is a God of increase. The first instruction He gave humans in Genesis 1 was for increase. *"God blessed them and said to them, be fruitful and increase...."* (GENESIS 1:28)

God does not want to withhold anything from you, but he wants to overload you with His benefits. Day by day, week by week, month by month you will be set free and receive the abundant things of God.

A Thousand Times More!

There are many Christians living in the land of "not enough", "barely enough", or "never enough" and all the time God wants us living in the land of "more than enough". God wants to show us Favor. I hope you are getting this in your spirit man. This is the rising of a new day for you. I am not talking about where you have been or how far you have come. I am talking about where you are about to go to become a thousand times more than you are right now.

A Day of Favor Will Change Your Life Forever.

I like the way Dr. Mike Murdock says it, "A day of Favor is worth 1,000 days of labor." You can't work enough to get everything you want. You can't work enough hours or jobs to get everything you are going to need. You have to have God's Favor.

Favor will cause you to rise to the top!

Again we can look at the life of Joseph. His dad had given him a coat of many colors. It was a coat of Favor. He was so excited about this Favor that he wanted to go down to the fields and show it to his brothers.

Let me tell you right now that not everyone is going to be as excited as you are when you receive Favor. Everyone does not become overjoyed when you get blessed. I mean this was Joseph's own family. He went to his brothers and said, "Look at the coat dad gave me…it's my coat of Favor." His brothers, his own family, took the coat off of him, beat him up, threw him in a pit, and sold him as a slave. That was his family.

I know you are sitting there thinking "that doesn't sound like Favor to me." Having Favor doesn't mean you won't have problems. It just means problems won't have you because you will rise above them. Joseph did that exact thing. He rose back to the top.

He became a slave in Potiphar's house. Potiphar gave him the keys to the car, the credit cards, and the checkbook and said, "you run the house." The Bible says that Potiphar's house was blessed because Joseph was in charge.

"The Lord was with Joseph and he prospered, and he lived in the house of his Egyptian master. When his master saw that the Lord was with him and that the Lord gave him success in everything he did, Joseph found Favor in his eyes and became his attendant. Potiphar put him in charge of his household, and he entrusted to his care everything he owned. From the time he put him in charge of his household and of all that he owned, the Lord blessed the household of the Egyptian because of Joseph. The blessing of the Lord was on everything Potiphar had, both in the house and in the field." (Genesis 39:2-5)

When you really understand the Favor of God you will understand that the people you work for will be blessed because you work for them.

Well, he ran into a little misunderstanding because of Potiphar's wife and ended up in prison. There went his Favor. Not exactly. The Bible says that the warden started putting Joseph in charge of things at the prison. The Bible also says that as long as Joseph was in charge, the warden did not even worry. Again he rose to the top.

"But while Joseph was there in prison, the Lord was with him; he showed him kindness and granted him favor in the eyes of the prison warden. So the warden put Joseph in charge of all those held in the prison, and he was made responsible for all that was done there. The warden paid no attention to anything under Joseph's care, because the Lord was with Joseph and gave him success in whatever he did."
(GENESIS 39:20-23)

While in prison, he interpreted a dream for Pharaoh. Pharaoh took him from the prison and brought him to the palace. In 24 hours, he went from being a prisoner to being the second in command of the nation.

"Then Pharaoh said to Joseph, 'Since God has made all this known to you, there is no one so discerning and wise as you. You shall be in charge of my palace, and all my people are to submit to your orders.

Only with respect to the throne will I be greater than you.' So Pharaoh said to Joseph, 'I hereby put you in charge of the whole land of Egypt.' Then Pharaoh took his signet ring from his finger and put it on Joseph's finger. He dressed him in robes of fine linen and put a gold chain around his neck. He had him ride in a chariot as his second-in-command, and men shouted before him, 'Make way!' Thus he put him in charge of the whole land of Egypt." (GENESIS 41:39-43)

Favor will accelerate your destiny in life.

The things that may have taken you 10 years to do in the past will only take 1 year. The things that took a year will only take a few weeks, and the things that took a few weeks will only take a few hours. Your life could drastically change in the next 24 hours.

Joseph was in prison one day, and the next day he was in the palace. His life totally changed in just a matter of hours. God is no respecter of person, and He can do the same thing for you.

I want you to stop whatever you are doing…sit down…and read this book. You will discover keys to increasing your Favor. I believe it will change your life, and help you to realize that you are blessed and highly favored of the Father.

You are God's Favorite!
DAVE MARTIN

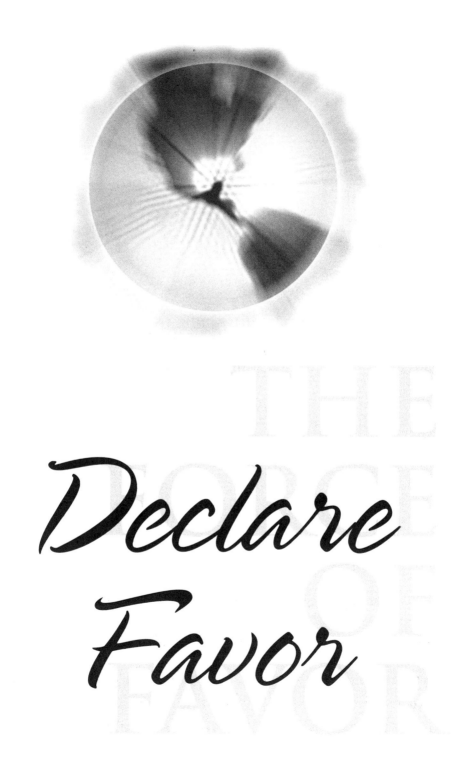

Declare
Favor

CHAPTER ONE

Declare Favor

T his is a very important chapter, if not the most important chapter in this book. The words of our mouth, our confessions, are powerful.

In the book of Proverbs, it says that the tongue has the power of life and death. You have to learn to declare Favor over your life on a daily basis.

SIX AREAS WHERE YOU WILL NEED FAVOR

1 *Declare Favor with your family.*

Favor has saved many marriages and restored many relationships. If there are situations in your home and family, that you do not know how to handle or what to do, begin to declare the Favor of God in that situation. Refuse to accept any negative report. Take charge of the situation by declaring Favor in your family. Declare that your wife loves you, and you love your wife. Declare that your husband loves you, and you love your husband. If your spouse or children are unsaved, declare that the Favor of God will give you a way, or send someone into their life, to show them the love of God.

2 *Christine and I declare Favor when we are traveling.*

When you travel the way that we do, you are always meeting new people and coming into situations where you need Favor. When we arrive in a city or at a new church, we always declare favor with the people. We always agree together that God will show us favor with them and help us to teach them how they, too, can walk in the Favor of God.

It is exciting to live with the expectation of good things happening to you. There are always situations in traveling where God can show you Favor. We had ended several days of meetings in the Seattle area and was scheduled to fly back to Dallas the next morning, when I discovered that there was a flight that left that night at 11:50pm. We were ready to get home. So we decided that we would try to change to that flight.

I called the airline to find out the availability for that flight. They told me that the flight was full and to go on that flight we would be changing the day of our travel. There would be a $75 fee per person. I told Christine what they said, and we decided to declare Favor and go to the airport. We joined hands on the way and thanked God for Favor that some how we would be able to get on the flight.

When we arrived at the airport to check in, the lady told us that the flight was full. But if we wanted, she would put us on the standby list. We said that would be great. She also told us that since we were only ten minutes from the day we were scheduled to fly, she would wave the $75 change fee for us. FAVOR! We got to the gate and found out that we were numbers seven and eight on the list of standbys.

They began to load the plane, and we sat there waiting to find out if there would be room. After several minutes they began to call people from the standby list. They called the first few quickly, then they called the next couple of names. We sat there knowing that we had declared Favor in the situation and expecting our names to be called. A man came off the plane and went to the counter and was speaking to the person there. We heard him say that there were only two seats left on the plane, and that they would go ahead and fill it up.

Of course the last two seats were for Christine and me. They called us to the counter and made us aware that they were sorry to tell us (and hoped we didn't mind) but the only two seats left were in First Class. We let them know that we didn't mind, and we boarded the plane headed fo our First Class seats. I don't know if you have ever sat in First Class, but it is Favor.

I remember for years wondering what would happen when they closed that curtain in First Class. What was happening up there? What are they doing? They have real silverware, and the food is hot. It is amazing…a little bit of heaven on earth.

That is just one example of the Favor wc have received as we declare it in different situations. I want to encourage you to expect good things to happen to you. Many times in my life I have received Favor without knowing to declare and confess it; but since learning this principle, it has increased many times over. The Force of Favor is an incredible benefit we have as a child of God.

3 *You need to declare Favor in all your dealings with man.*

That is in your business with your neighbors, in the store, and on your job. If you have your own business, then you will need Favor with clients and prospective clients. You need Favor with your employees. You need to declare it over your entire business.

When you are going to purchase a house or car, you need God's Favor going before you to prepare the way so that you can get the best deal.

4 *You need Favor with your neighbors.*

I remember one evening when Christine and I returned home from over two weeks of meetings. We were tired and excited to be home. Our neighbors happened to be outside grilling some chicken for dinner when we returned. They asked us about our trip and the success of the meetings. We said goodnight and went inside to unpack. In a few minutes there was a knock on the door, and it was our neighbor with a platter of grilled chicken and vegetables. We were tired, and didn't know what we were going to do for dinner. Thank God for Favor with our neighbors.

5 *You need Favor on your job because Favor will determine your income.*

Favor with your employer can put you in position for a raise or promotion. You may be looking for a job and need Favor on your interviews. You can go to your interview declaring you probably won't get the job...you're not qualified...you don't have enough experience...and you probably won't get the job. On the other hand you can go in declaring God's Favor...that you are His favorite...and you can expect to get the job. Even though you might not be the most qualified, you will get the job.

6 *You need to declare Favor in the store.*

There have been times that I needed to run in the store to get something, and I was in a hurry. I picked up what I needed and went to the check-out line, and they were all full. I began to declare Favor. "Father, I am in a hurry tonight. Could you show me Favor by opening line four?" You know it is usually only seconds, and someone walks up and says, "Sir, I'll take you right over here." That is God's favor.

I want you to take a minute and repeat this Favor Declaration that we declare over our life everyday.

"Lord, I thank you today for Favor. I thank you that I am your favorite child, and that means I am particularly esteemed and have undue preference I am the apple of your eye I am crowned with glory and honor; and because I wear a crown, that shows me that I am royalty. I have the character and status of a king. As part of the royal family, I can expect preferential treatment. I declare today Favor in every area of my life…with my family on my job, with my neighbors, in the market place, and in places where I will travel. I am choosing to accept and walk in the Favor of God."

THE

FORCE

Obedience

OF

FAVOR

CHAPTER TWO

Obedience

Favor is a reward for obedience.

I believe that God rewards you when you obey an instruction He gives you. *"If you are willing and obedient, you will eat the best of the land."* (ISAIAH 1:19)

If you are going to ask God to increase Favor in your life, then your lifestyle must be pleasing to him. I believe that your obedience determines the amount of Favor you receive. Your behavior and your conduct must be pleasing to Him.

Favor is a reward for obedience.

I heard the testimony of a farmer who lived in the Dallas area that is a perfect example of what I am talking about here. This farmer was a regular church attender, a tither, and knew the voice of God when he spoke. He would always do his best to obey God's voice.

One day this farmer was out in his fields plowing, and the Holy Spirit spoke to him and said, "Go to the back corner of your property and dig for oil." Well this farmer thought to himself that there is no oil within 100 miles of here, and he kept plowing. Again the Holy Spirit spoke to him to go to the back corner of his property and dig for oil.

This man knew the voice of God and decided to obey. He hired the men he needed and got together the equipment and began to dig for oil. The people thought that this man was crazy. I guess it was probably like the people mocking Noah for building an ark when there was no rain. The thing was…they were not laughing for long.

There will be times when God gives you a command that others think (and you may think) is crazy. But He will reward you for your obedience.

It was just two days after they had begun to dig that they struck oil. The oil well began to produce about 600 barrels of oil each day. Oil was selling at that time for about $41 per barrel. If you figure that up it comes out to about $24,600 of daily backyard income. How would you like to make almost $25,000 a day for listening and obeying a command from God?

Favor is a reward for obedience.

The farmer had no idea that there was oil within 100 miles of his property. He was simply willing and obedient to the Holy Spirit, and now he is eating the best of the land. That is…the best houses, the best cars, the best clothes, and the best of the land.

He now has ten oil wells that are producing an average of 2000 barrels per day. I would say that is pretty good pay for walking in faith and being willing and obedient to do what God asks you to do. He may ask you to do some things that seem illogical, but the rewards for your obedience will be great.

"The earth is the Lord's, and everything in it, the world, and all who live in it." (PSALMS 24:1) That includes what is on top of the earth and what is underneath the earth. The cattle on a thousand hills, and the hills are His.

"For every animal of the forest is mine, and the cattle on a thousand hills." (PSALMS 50:10) The silver and the gold are His, and even the oil is the Lord's. *"The silver is mine and the gold is mine, declares the Lord Almighty."* (HAGGAI 2:8)

Obedience is the only thing that God ever requires. Your only responsibility is 24-hours of obedience. Your focus should be 24-hours of hourly obedience. This will launch you into new levels of increase.

EIGHT FACTS ABOUT OBEDIENCE

1 Obedience is doing anything God commands you to do, regardless of the cost.

2 Your obedience guarantees that God will always respond in Favor to your requests.

3 Promotion always follows your obedience.

4 Your obedience to God's instruction is the only proof of your love for Him.

5 Your obedience is rewarded with supernatural protection.

6 Your obedience to your employer guarantees rewards from God.

7 Your obedience to rely totally on the Word of God creates increased Favor.

8 Provision is only guaranteed at your place of obedience.

Find
God

CHAPTER THREE

Find God

Finding Him is a key to increasing in God's Favor. The more intimate you are with God the more of His Favor you will experience.

"Now then, my sons, listen to me; blessed are those who keep my ways. Listen to my instruction and be wise; do not ignore it. Blessed is the man who listens to me, watching daily at my doors, waiting at my doorway. For whoever finds me finds life and receives Favor from the Lord."

(PROVERBS 8:32-35)

How do you become more intimate with Him? You do this by spending time in the Word and in prayer. You must spend time with Him on a daily basis if you want to grow closer to Him.

You need to spend time in the Word every day. I used to say that it didn't matter when you read your Bible as long as you did it sometime each day. I now believe that you need to do it first thing in the morning. The Word of God is your road map, and every day is a trip. Would you ever go on a trip, and when you return read the map? Of course you wouldn't. You would read the map before you left so that you would know which way to go. The Word of God will give you direction for each day. You may read something in the morning, and not really understand what it has to do with you. But later that day you find yourself in a situation and you think back to what you read and there is your answer.

If you left for a trip and never read the map, you may find yourself at a crossroad and not know which way to go. But if you had looked at the map, you would know exactly what to do. You will encounter these same types of things in life. You may find yourself at a crossroad and not know what decision to make. But if you have read your spiritual road map that day, you will know exactly what direction to go.

You must also spend time in prayer. Prayer is simply talking to God. You have to take time to talk to Him every day. If I do not take the time to talk to my wife on a daily basis, then my relationship with her would never grow. During your prayer time, it is also important to take time to listen and let him talk to you. If all I did was talk to my wife and never let her say anything back to me, we would never develop intimacy in our relationship.

If you want to have intimacy in your relationship with God, then your prayer time will have to be a two-way communication. That means you will talk to Him and give Him time to talk to you. You may be needing an answer and never get it because you never give Him time to respond.

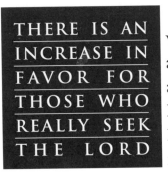

THERE IS AN INCREASE IN FAVOR FOR THOSE WHO REALLY SEEK THE LORD

There is an increase in Favor for those who really seek the Lord. Peter, James, and John were always drawing near and they experienced a higher level of Favor than the rest of the disciples. Draw near to Him and you, too, can receive an increase in Favor.

I believe that there are different levels of Favor. You can move to increased levels of Favor when you move into His inner circle. It is just like in the natural. I have worked for various large ministries, and I have found that the closer you are to the inner circle (those closest to the man of God) the more you will receive a higher level of Favor.

The closer you are to someone the more willing they are to show you Favor.

There is promotion and prosperity for those who seek the Lord.

"I love those who love me, and those who seek me find me. With me are riches and honor, enduring wealth and prosperity. My fruit is better than fine gold; What I yield surpasses choice silver. I walk in the way of righteousness, along the paths of justice, bestowing wealth on those who love me and making their treasuries full."

(PROVERBS 8:17-21)

Riches and honor come to those who seek the Lord. Let God make you a success by showing you an increase in Favor as you seek Him. I want you to believe God today for the impossible in your life. The only limitation that you have is your lack of understanding God's laws.

You can live in the land of promise today. You can live in a land of increase. A land where milk and honey flow. A land of Favor. You just have to get up and take it by faith. *"Those who seek the Lord lack no good thing."* (PROVERBS 34:10)

If you will begin to expect favor to flow in your life, then you can have it today. You receive Favor by faith just like you would anything else. Every country has its own currency. America has the dollar, Mexico has the peso, Japan has the yen, and the list goes on. I believe that heaven has its own currency as well.

Heaven's currency is Faith.

The Bible tells us that anything we need, we can get with our faith. You receive salvation by faith...you receive healing by faith...you receive financial blessings by faith...and you receive increased Favor by faith. If you will use your faith and seek Him like never before, you can expect an increase in Favor.

FAVOR
BLESSING
INCREASE

THE
FORCE
OF
FAVOR

Excellence

CHAPTER FOUR

Excellence

Excellence is doing the best you can with what you have.

The dictionary says that excellence is the state of excelling in anything. I believe excellence is also going the extra mile. The phrase "going the extra mile" is another way to say excellence.

There is a lot of traffic on the first mile, but the moment you get to the second mile (or the extra mile) there is hardly any one out there.

God does not want us to do just enough to get by. He is not the God of "good enough;" He is the God of "more than enough."

As Christians we should be the hardest workers on the job, not the ones waiting by the timeclock at 4:59pm to punch out and go home. You know it is not the unemployment rate that shocks me, it is the employment rate that shocks me. I cannot believe that so many lazy people can keep jobs.

I went into a shoe store the other day and told the man I was looking for some loafers. He said, "Okay, one is in the back, and the other one is at lunch." If we want to walk in the Favor of God, then we have to give an honest days work for an honest day's pay. We should be the one setting the example for work ethics.

A strong work ethic is one of the most important things a winner must possess. The only place that excellence comes before work is in the dictionary. People of excellence do not see work as a negative thing, but a positive thing that results in an increase of Favor.

The former prime minister of Great Britain, Margaret Thatcher once said, "I do not know anyone who has gotten to the top without hard work."

You may need to stay late to get a project done. You might need to skip lunch to make sure things are in order. I promise you that going the extra mile will increase the Favor you have with your employer, and that will increase your income.

Excellence is giving more than is expected of you.

Lee Iacocca said, "The kind of people that I look for to fill top management positions are the eager beavers, people who try to do more than they are expected to do—they always reach." This should be our goal in every area of our life…wanting to do more than just the average.

THE KEY TO YOUR FUTURE IS HIDDEN IN YOUR DAILY ROUTINE

Dr. Mike Murdock says, "The key to your future is hidden in your daily routine." You have to start your day in full gear not in neutral. There is no better time than now.

God's desire for us is that we do the best we can in every situation.

We cannot expect God to increase us in Favor, or in any other area, if we are not willing to do our best.

You can't expect God to give you a new car, if you can' keep clean the one you have. You can't expect God to give you a new house, if you can't keep clean the one you have You can't expect God to give you new clothes, if you don' iron the ones you already have.

I said earlier that excellence is doing the best you can with what you have. This is where many people miss it They are looking at someone else's level of excellence and trying to compare, when God hasn't moved them to tha level yet.

Pastor Robb Thompson has been the greatest example of excellence in my life and ministry. I have learned so much just by watching him in different situations. I have seen him walk down the halls of his church, and point out a small scratch on a wall, and it will be fixed within hours.

He has taught the people around him to be people of excellence. Whether it is the church, his house, his car, or the clothes he wears....I have never seen him not doing his best. I have told pastors across this country that if they want to see true excellence, then they need to make their way to Chicago and visit Pastor Robb Thompson and Family Harvest Church.

Excellence will increase your Favor with God and with man.

"Whatever your hand finds to do, do it with all your might." (ECCLESIASTES 9:10)

FAVOR
BLESSING
INCREASE

Solve a Problem for Someone

CHAPTER FIVE

Solve a Problem for Someone

Solving a problem for someone is one of the quickest ways to increase your Favor.

I want you to begin to look for a problem that you can solve for someone. It may be your spouse, your boss, or your pastor. If you will begin to solve problems for someone, it will increase your Favor.

Find the problem that *you* are the answer to.

The higher levels of Favor will be determined by the problems you are willing to solve. Everyone has a problem. The Favor you receive will depend on the willingness you have to solve a problem for someone else.

You were created to solve a problem.

You are the answer to a problem for somebody.

FOUR WAYS SOLVING A PROBLEM WILL INCREASE YOUR FAVOR

1 *Solve a problem better than anyone else.*

There is a particular lady that I go to for my alterations. I have bought suits in other cities, and instead of letting them alter it, I will bring it back to Dallas. She knows what I like, and she does it better than anyone else.

2 *Solve a problem faster than anyone else.*

When I need to have pictures developed, I like to get them fast. I will pass a couple of places that develop pictures, including a one-hour photo lab. Why? Because just on the other side of the hour photo lab is a half-hour photo lab.

3 *Solve a problem with a good attitude.*

This is one of the first characteristics that the top CEO's and pastors use when looking for employees—people who can keep a good and healthy attitude in the middle of adversity. People who can accomplish the good in a hostile environment without losing their cool. We have all heard it before, *"Your attitude determines your altitude."*

4 *Always be willing to solve a problem.*

I am sure that you have heard someone at some point and time, say, "That is not in my job description." This phrase is not in the vocabulary of a person who is increasing Favor in their life. If you truly want to increase your Favor, you will always be willing to do what needs to be done for the success of the company or ministry.

Problems are a catalyst for Favor.

I remember the first time I met Dr. Mike Murdock. I had gone to Dallas with Rodney Howard-Browne for a meeting that he was having. While I was in Dallas I went to visit a friend of mine who was working for Dr. Murdock.

I was introduced to Dr. Murdock in the middle of a discussion he was having with a couple of his employees. They were discussing a date that he needed to be in Florida. I heard the discussion and decided to see if I could help by solving a problem.

I went into the other office and picked up the phone and called my friend and father in the Lord, Dr. Dan White. Dr. White pastors Jacksonville Christian Center in Jacksonville, Florida. This happened to be the area where Dr. Murdock needed to be. I asked Dr. White if he would be interested in having Dr. Murdock minister at his church, and he said he would.

We looked at the dates, and Dr. White said, "Let's put it on the calendar." I went back into the other room where Dr. Murdock and his staff were discussing a couple of different options. I said, "Dr. Murdock, I have a friend who pastors a great church in that area, and he would love for you to come that day."

I solved a problem for Dr. Murdock that has brought me much favor. I was scheduled to go back to Tampa with Rodney on Saturday when Dr. Murdock asked me to go with him to Cleveland, Ohio. I agreed and ended up spending the next three months going everywhere Dr. Murdock went.

I solved a problem for him that has produced more favor for my life and ministry than any other problem I have solved. I did Dr. Murdock's scheduling for the next three years, and Christine and I have had the opportunity to travel around the world learning the ministry from one of the greatest evangelist of our day.

If that is not Favor, I don't know what is!

FAVOR
BLESSING
INCREASE

THE
FORCE OF
FAVOR

A Gift

CHAPTER SIX

A Gift

A gift will increase Favor.

I am sure that you have noticed that when the president visits another country, or a diplomat from another country visits America, they will bring with them a gift. A gift will increase Favor. *"A gift opens the way for the giver and ushers him into the presence of the great"* (PROVERBS 18:16)

I remember hearing this scripture growing up and was always taught that this was talking about a spiritual gift or talent given to us by God. If we would use our gifts, then God would promote us. He would put us before great men.

I have since found that this is not true. The gift that being talked about in this scripture is literally talking about a material gift. It is saying that if you will bring a material gift it will promote you, and you will find Favor.

Christine and I will often bring a gift to the pastor where we are ministering. Now, you do not bring a gift to manipulate, but to honor. If you gain a friendship or Favor by manipulation, then you will have to continue to manipulate to keep the friendship or Favor. We bring gifts in order to honor and thank the pastor for the opportunity to minister to those whom God has entrusted to him.

When the wise men came to give honor to the baby Jesus, they brought with them gifts.

"On coming to the house, they saw the child with his mother Mary, and they bowed down and worshipped him. Then they opened their treasures and presented him with gifts of gold and of incense and of myrrh." (MATTHEW 2:11)

THE
FORCE
Seed
OF
FAVOR

CHAPTER SEVEN

Seed

*If you will follow God's laws of sowing,
you will increase your Favor.*

**"Will a man rob God? Yet you rob me. But you ask,
'How do we rob you?' In tithes and offerings.
You are under a curse—the whole nation of you—
because you are robbing. Bring the whole tithe into
the storehouse, that there may be food in my house.
Test me in this,' says the Lord Almighty, and see
if I will not throw open the floodgates of heaven
and pour out so much blessing that you will
not have room enough for it."** (MALACHI 3:8-10)

The tithe will bring you into obedience with God's laws and put you in line for increased Favor.

The first thing we will talk about is the tithe. The tithe means tenth. When we tithe we are giving back to God

10% of our income as proof and evidence that we honor God as our provider. *"Honor the Lord with your wealth, with the firstfruits of all your crops; then your barns will be filled to overflowing, and your vats will brim over with new wine."* (PROVERBS 3:9-10)

When you keep the tithe you are stealing.

Stealing is taking that which belongs to another.

"You shall not steal." (EXODUS 20:15) I have seen people keep their tithe and use it to buy a new car. They are driving a stolen car. I have seen people use their tithe to buy a new suit and come to church on Sunday wearing that brand new stolen suit.

There are not a lot of people who will say it, but the Word says that thieves will not enter the kingdom of heaven. If you are not tithing, you are a thief. Are you so unthankful for the 90% God permits you to keep that you need to steal the other 10%.

I asked a congregation the other day, "When you bring your tithe, your 10%, how much do you have left?" Everyone said 90%. I told them, "Actually, you have a 100% left. The 10% was never really yours anyway. So you still have the entire amount that belongs to you."

Do not steal the tithe.

Tithing is your door to financial Favor.

Tithing shows that you have faith in the Word of God. When you write your tithe check, it is proof that you believe God. As you begin to tithe consistently, the Favor of God will begin to consistently flow into your life.

Your tithe and your seed will create a momentum for you. You have to sow with regularity if you want to reap with regularity. If you sow sporadically you will reap sporadically.

The word says that God will rebuke the devourer for the tither. Tithing can break the financial curse on your life and family. When you do not tithe you are putting yourself under a curse. But begin to tithe and watch God move.

When I was pastoring in Florida, I would teach my church regularly on the principle of tithing. I shared with them that this is the only place in the Bible where God tells us to prove Him. That means give me a try, and see if I am not right.

I challenged my church to prove Him. I gave them money back guarantee. I told them that if they would tithe for 90 days consistently, and if God didn't begin to bless their lives and families, then I would give them all the money back. Sometimes you have to step out in faith, and that is what I did.

Do you know that not one person asked me for the money back? We began to hear testimony after testimony of God's goodness. People began to be blessed and to prosper.

I want to encourage you, if you are not a tither, to start today. You may need to get up right now and go take a check to the church. I am telling you that He said, *"...prove me and see..."* He will open the windows of Heaven and pour out a blessing that I would not have room enough to contain.

I don't know about you, but I have never had a blessing yet that I could not contain. Do you know what that means? It means that there is more out there than I have received. I have not even come close to tapping into all the benefits of a tither. I want to encourage you to start tithing today.

The Word of God says that there is tithe and offering. I know in my life, growing up, I always heard about the tithe and offering. The only thing was, I never knew the incredible difference between the two. In the next few pages I want to share with you some life changing truths.

First, let me show you the difference between the tithe and the offering.

Every seed contains an invisible instruction.

If you were to look deep inside of a tomato seed you would find an instruction to produce a tomato. Orange seeds contain an instruction to produce oranges. You can not see it with the natural eye, but it is obviously there.

God decided the harvest when He created the seed.

I can still remember the night I caught this revelation, and it sank into my spirit. Dr. Mike Murdock was teaching, and he said these words. "When God wanted a family, He sowed His Son. He gave His Son an assignment to seek and save the lost. Jesus was the best seed God ever planted on earth. He contained an assignment, an instruction, and a purpose. Everything he did was connected to that assignment every day of His life."

I saw it. Even God would sow a seed for a specific harvest. Well, if it worked for God, I thought I should try it. I did. It worked, and my life has never been the same again. If, in these next few paragraphs, you can get a hold of this principle, it will change your life also.

In 2 Samuel 24, we see where David aimed his seed like an arrow. He gave it an instruction. He focused his faith and expected the desired result. Thousands were dead and David brought an offering for a specific thing, and the plague was stopped.

I love the story in 1 Kings 17, about the widow at Zarephath. The prophet gave her a picture of what God would do for her if she would give him something to eat. She saw the photograph of her harvest before she sowed her seed. She was sowing for a specific harvest.

**"For this is what the Lord, the God of Israel, says:
The jar of flour will not be used up and the
jug of oil will not run dry until the day
the Lord gives rain on the land.'"**(1 KINGS 17:14)

You always have a seed that can move you out of your present situation. Your seed may be your way out of trouble. I have sown seeds for healing, for Favor, for finances, for victory, for marriage, and many more. You know, you can't buy a miracle from God. I am not trying to tell you that, but you can sow a seed with expectation for a desired result.

Now this is what I want you to do. I am going to give you an opportunity to plant a Seed. I want you to listen to the voice of the Holy Spirit, and obey what He says. I then want you to name that Seed where you need God to show you Favor the most. He may speak to you about $10, $100, $1,000 or even more. Now I want you to take a step of faith and prove God with an offering. I challenge you right now to send $111 (DEUTERONOMY 1:11). Maybe you can send more, or maybe you can't send that much. But you can do something.

A seed of nothing will produce a season of nothing.

When you give, you are not buying from God. You are worshipping Him through your giving which shows Him that He is your Source. Christine and I want to agree with you for your miracle. I have enclosed a special page in this book for you to write down the things you want God to do, the areas you want Him to show you Favor.

Send it to me today—RIGHT NOW! We want to pray the prayer of agreement with you. I look forward to hearing from you today.

DAVE AND CHRISTINE MARTIN
P.O. BOX 608150
ORLANDO, FL 32860

7-16-11 Sowed $111 to Tom Moffet

THE
FORCE
OF
FAVOR

Favor
Testimonies

Favor Testimonies

I want to share with you some powerful testimonies of people, just like you and me from around the country that have heard this principle and acted on it. In this chapter, your faith will be encouraged and strengthened as you read these testimonies.

"When you spoke at my church I sowed a seed for Favor. The next morning the stock market had a significant drop, and people lost thousands of dollars. My stock went up thousands. That is the Favor of God."

— SAN FRANCISCO, CA

"I am a builder who specializes in remodeling. We had two months that business was so slow and we didn't know what we were going to do. Less than a week after hearing your message on Favor and beginning to expect it, we signed jobs on three new houses."

— LITTLE ROCK, AR

"I had been on my job as a part time employee for just a couple of months. There were around 20 people waiting to go full time, and most of those people were ahead of me. I became a monthly Favor partner with your ministry, and the next week my boss called me in and asked if I would like to go full time. He said he would move me to the top of the list if I wanted him to. I said, 'of course I would.' It was only two weeks later that I was promoted to supervisor. The other supervisor had been with the company four years before becoming a supervisor, and I was made one in four months. Favor will accelerate your destiny. Thank you for teaching this powerful message."

— St. Petersburg, FL

"I had been trying to find a new job and had been for several interviews. You spoke on declaring Favor when you go for a job interview. I had an interview the next morning, and I decided to try it. It worked! I not only got the job, but more pay than I was asking for Praise the Lord for His Favor"

— Dallas, TX

"After being set free from drugs and getting involved with my church, I decided that I wanted to be an usher. I didn't have the money to go and buy several suits. So I thought I would just buy one, and that would be a start. My wife and I picked one out and took it to have alterations done. When we went back to pick it up the man at the alteration place asked me if I would like two more

suits. Someone had dropped them off over 90 days earlier and had never picked them up. They were both my exact size."

— IRVING, TX

"I was in one of your meetings and heard you talking about how you can receive Favor on your job. I decided to try it, and it worked. Less than five days after I sowed a Seed and wrote 'job promotion' on it, my boss called me in and told me he wanted to give me a promotion. Then he told me I was not only going to get a promotion, but I was going to get a raise as well. My salary just went from $25,000 to $43,000 a year. Thank God for His Favor!"

— TAMPA, FL

"My wife and I had a bill at our doctors office that we were trying to pay off. He had just built a new office building and needed landscaping done. I own a landscaping company and had thought about trading some landscaping for the bill we owed. Before I could ask, his office called me and asked if I would be interested in doing the landscaping at the new office for a trade out on our bill. Thank God for Favor!"

— PORTLAND, OR

"I had a school loan of $23,000 that I was trying to pay off. I had just made my first payment on this loan, but my desire was to pay it off quickly I wanted God to show me Favor in this situation. I planted a Seed when you were at our church and God moved quicker than I ever imagined.

Within five days I received a letter from the school loan company which stated that they had received my payment, and pending the processing of it, they were marking my billed paid in full. I couldn't believe it. $23,000 of debt canceled."

— ORLANDO, FL

"The first time that I heard you speak about the Favor of God I sowed a Seed into your ministry for Favor in a relationship I needed God to show me Favor and somehow bring restoration. God began to move; and in just a few short weeks, that relationship was restored and is growing stronger every day. Praise God! I believe in sowing Seed and especially in a ministry that is producing the kind of results you are."

— HUDSON, FL

"I had never thought about the Favor of God bringing healing to my body until you shared about Sarah in the Bible. I took ahold of that and ask God to show me Favor by healing my body. I had suffered with tremendous pain and arthritis in my legs and hips. I ask God to show me Favor and take this pain from me and heal me, and He did. Today I am totally healed, and there is no more pain."

— CHICAGO, IL

"My husband and I had been trying to have a child for years. We had been to clinics and tried everything. Then you came to our church and shared your message on Favor.

We had not tried that. We had prayed, but we had never asked God for Favor. Well that night you laid hands on us and prayed for God to show us Favor, and he did. I am now four months pregnant, and things are great. Thank you so much for being obedient to the Holy Spirit and sharing the message of Favor."

— DENVER, CO

"I had a debt of $1500 that I owed a man in my church. When you were ministering at our church, I decided to sow the $111 Seed that you were talking about even though I had several bills that I owed. I knew that $111 would not pay off my bills so I sowed it. I did that in the service that morning. After service that night the man who I owed walked up to me and said that God told him to forgive me of my debt."

— WHEATON, IL

"I had heard you preach at our church before, but never really believed all the stuff about sowing and reaping. The last time you were there something told me to try it and see what would happen. I gave an offering that night and within ten days there was $5000 directly deposited into our account. We thought it must have been a mistake, but later found out it was an inheritance from a relative who had died several years ago. I had forgotten they were still dealing with the estate. It works and thank you for sharing. From this day forward I will never doubt God's Favor."

— KOKOMO, IN

"When you were at our church I sowed a $111 Seed into your ministry My family was getting ready to make a move out of state and needed all the money we had. But we obeyed God and sowed. As soon as church was over, someone handed me a $111 check and said, 'God told me to give this to you.' After church we went out to eat with a family. By the end of our lunch, he had handed me ten, $100 bills. $1,000!!!! In less than three hours after my $111 Seed, God blessed me with $1,111."

— MONTGOMERY, AL

"I sowed a Seed for Favor on my business. We were just beginning and needed some customers. I had a meeting with a perspective customer the day after I sowed my Seed. I confessed Favor, and I walked out with the job."

— HICKORY, NC

"My business was doing well, and I was satisfied with my financial income. Then you came into my life and encouraged me to reach for increase and favor. Within a few weeks of sowing into your ministry, I got a new client that was worth one million dollars a year. That one client doubled the income of my entire company. I just met with them again last week, and they have raised there business with me from one million to three million dollars a year."

— IRVING, TX

"I had just moved to the states from Costa Rico with my family, when you came to our church. I had just found a job and a place to live. We needed furniture, but could not afford it at the time. I went to work the day after you laid hands on us, and my boss told me to take the truck and pick up some things. He told me where to go, and I went to the place. They filled my truck with new furniture, and I went back. My boss told me the furniture was for my family and me. Praise the Lord."

— HICKORY, NC

"I had a debt of $65,000 from a business deal that I had done. I didn't feel that I owed this money, and it was not right. I spoke with the bank, and they told me they would research it. I was in one of your Favor Friday meetings and planted a $1,000 seed for Favor in this situation. Within ten days I received a call from the Vice President of the bank. He said there had been a mistake. I did not owe the bank $65,000, but they actually owed me $27,600. They cut the check that day and overnighted it."

— ORLANDO, FL

Favor Memory Scriptures

Favor Memory Scriptures

In this section you will find 52 Scriptures. One scripture on Favor for you to memorize every week of the year

WEEK 1
"But Abel brought fat portions from some of the firstborn of the flock. The Lord looked with Favor on Abel and his offering." (GENESIS 4:4)

WEEK 2
"So the Lord said, "I will wipe mankind, whom I have created, from the face of the earth—men and animals, and creatures that move along the ground, and birds of the air—for I am grieved that I have made them." But Noah found Favor in the eyes of the Lord." (GENESIS 6:7,8)

WEEK 3

"He said, 'If I have found Favor in your eyes, my lord, do not pass your servant by. Let a little water be brought, and then you may all wash your feet and rest under this tree. Let me get you something to eat, so you can be refreshed and then go on your way—now that you have come to your servant.' Very well, they answered, do as you say." (GENESIS 18:3-5)

WEEK 4

"The Lord was with Joseph and he prospered, and he lived in the house of his Egyptian master. When his master saw that the Lord was with him and that the Lord gave him success in everything he did, Joseph found Favor in his eyes and became his attendant. Potiphar put him in charge of his household, and he entrusted to his care everything he owned. From the time he put him in charge of his household and of all that he owned, the Lord blessed the household of the Egyptian because of Joseph. The blessing of the Lord was on everything Potiphar had, both in the house and in the field. So he left in Joseph's care everything he had; with Joseph in charge, he did not concern himself with anything except the food he ate." (GENESIS 39:2-6)

WEEK 5

"Joseph's master took him and put him in prison, the place where the king's prisoners were confined. But while Joseph was there in the prison, the Lord was with him. He showed him kindness and granted him Favor in the eyes of the prison warden. So the warden put Joseph in charge of all those held in the prison, and he was made responsible for all that was done there. The warden paid no attention to anything under Joseph's care, because the Lord was with Joseph and gave him success in whatever he did." (GENESIS 39:20-23)

WEEK 6

"And I will make the Egyptians Favorably disposed toward this people, so that when you leave you will not go empty handed." (EXODUS 3:21)

WEEK 7

"The Lord made the Egyptians Favorably disposed toward the people, and Moses himself was highly regarded in Egypt by Pharaoh's officials and by the people." (EXODUS 11:3)

WEEK 8

"The Lord had made the Egyptians Favorably disposed toward the people, and they gave them what they asked for; so they plundered the Egyptians." (EXODUS 12:36)

WEEK 9

"Moses said to the Lord, "You have been telling me, 'Lead these people,' but you have not let me know whom you will send with me. You have said, 'I know you by name and you have found Favor with me.' If I have found Favor in your eyes, teach me your ways so I may know you and continue to find Favor with you. Remember that this nation is your people." (EXODUS 33:12,13)

WEEK 10

"O Lord, if I have found Favor in your eyes, he said, then let the Lord go with us...then the Lord said:'I am making a covenant with you. Before all your people I will do wonders never before done in any nation in all the world. The people you live among will see how awesome is the work that I, the Lord, will do for you.'" (EXODUS 34:9,10)

WEEK 11

"I will look on you with Favor and make you fruitful and increase your numbers, and I will keep my covenant with you." (LEVITICUS 26:9)

WEEK 12

"The Lord bless you and keep you; the Lord make his face shine upon you and be gracious to you; the Lord turn his face toward you and give you peace." (NUMBERS 6:24-26)

WEEK 13

"Gideon replied, 'If now I have found Favor in your eyes, give me a sign that it is really you talking to me. Please do not go away until I come back with an offering and set it before you.' And the Lord said, 'I will wait until you return.'" (JUDGES 6:17,18)

WEEK 14

"At this, she bowed down with her face to the ground. She exclaimed, 'Why have I found such Favor in your eyes that you notice me'…. 'May I continue to find favor in your eyes, my lord,' she said. 'You have given me comfort and have spoken kindly to your servant.'" (RUTH 2:10,13)

WEEK 15

"And the boy Samuel continued to grow in stature and in Favor with the Lord and with men." (1 SAMUEL 2:26)

WEEK 16

"May the Lord now show you kindness and faithfulness, and I too will show you the same Favor because you have done this." (2 SAMUEL 2:6)

WEEK 17

"Then Jehoahaz sought the Lord's Favor, and the Lord listened to him." (2 KINGS 13:4)

WEEK 18

"In his distress he sought the Favor of the Lord his God and humbled himself greatly before the God of his fathers." (2 CHRONICLES 33:12)

WEEK 19

"When the turn came for Esther (the girl Mordecai had adopted, the daughter of his uncle Abihail) to go to the king, she asked for nothing other than what Hegai, the king's eunuch who was in charge of the harem, suggested. And Esther won the Favor of everyone who saw her." (ESTHER 2:15)

WEEK 20

"Then Queen Esther answered, 'If I have found Favor with you, O king, and if it pleases your majesty, grant me my life—this is my petition. And spare my people—this is my request.'" (ESTHER 7:3)

WEEK 21

"He prays to God and finds Favor with him, he sees God's face and shouts for joy; he is restored by God to his righteous state." (JOB 33:26)

WEEK 22

"Many are asking, 'Who can show us any good?' Let the light of your face shine upon us, O Lord." (PSALMS 4:6)

WEEK 23

'For surely, O Lord, you bless the righteous; you surround them with your Favor as with a shield." (PSALMS 5:12)

WEEK 24

"For his anger lasts only a moment, but his Favor lasts a lifetime; weeping may remain for a night, but rejoicing comes in the morning." (PSALMS 30:5)

WEEK 25

"Let your face shine on your servant; save me in your unfailing love." (PSALMS 31:16)

WEEK 26

"The king is enthralled by your beauty; honor him, for he is your lord. The Daughter of Tyre will come with a gift, men of wealth will seek your Favor." (PSALMS 45:11,12)

WEEK 27

"May God be gracious to us and bless us and make his face shine upon us." (PSALMS 67:1)

WEEK 28

"Restore us, O God; make your face shine upon us, that we may be saved." (PSALM 80:3)

WEEK 29

"You showed Favor to your land, O Lord; you restored the fortunes of Jacob." (PSALMS 85:1)

WEEK 30

"For you are their glory and strength, and by your Favor you exalt our horn." (PSALMS 87:17)

WEEK 31

"May the Favor of the Lord our God rest upon us; establish the work of our hands for us — yes, establish the work of our hands." (Psalms 90:17)

WEEK 32

"You will arise and have compassion on Zion, for it is time to show Favor to her; the appointed time has come." (PSALMS 102:13)

WEEK 33

"Make your face shine upon your servant and teach me your decrees." (PSALMS 119:135)

WEEK 34

"Let love and faithfulness never leave you; bind them around your neck, write them on the tablet of your heart. Then you will win Favor and a good name in the sight of God and man." (PROVERBS 3:3,4)

WEEK 35

"Now then, my sons, listen to me; blessed are those who keep my ways. Listen to my instruction and be wise; do not ignore it. Blessed is the man who listens to me, watching daily at my doors, waiting at my doorway. For whoever finds me finds life and receives Favor from the Lord." (PROVERBS 8:32-35)

WEEK 36

"A good man obtains Favor from the Lord, but the Lord condemns a crafty man." (PROVERBS 12:2)

WEEK 37

"Good understanding wins Favor, but the way of the unfaithful is hard." (PROVERBS 13:15)

WEEK 38

"He who finds a wife finds what is good and receives Favor from the Lord." (PROVERBS 18:22)

WEEK 39

"Many curry Favor with a ruler, and everyone is the friend of a man who gives gifts." (PROVERBS 19:6)

WEEK 40

"Yet the Lord longs to be gracious to you; he rises to show you Favor. For the Lord is a God of justice. Blessed are all who wait for him!" (ISAIAH 30:18)

WEEK 41

"Foreigners will rebuild your walls, and their kings will serve you. Though in anger I struck you, in Favor I will show you compassion. Your gates will always stand open, they will never be shut, day or night, so that men may bring you the wealth of the nations." (ISAIAH 60:10,11)

WEEK 42

"The Spirit of the Sovereign Lord is on me, because the Lord has anointed me to preach good news to the poor. He has sent me to bind up the brokenhearted, to proclaim freedom for the captives and release for the prisoners, to proclaim the year of the Lord's Favor." (ISAIAH 61:1,2)

WEEK 43

"But Daniel resolved not to defile himself with the royal food and wine, and he asked the chief official for permission not to defile himself this way. Now God has caused the official to show Favor and sympathy to Daniel." (DANIEL 1:8,9)

WEEK 44

"The angel went to her and said, 'Greetings, you who are highly Favored! The Lord is with you.' Mary was greatly troubled at his words and wondered what kind of greeting this might be. But the angel said to her, 'Do not be afraid, Mary, you have found Favor with God.'" (LUKE 1:28-30)

WEEK 45

"Glory to God in the highest, and on earth peace to men on whom his Favor rests." (LUKE 2:14)

WEEK 46

"And Jesus grew in wisdom and stature, and in Favor with God and men." (LUKE 2:52)

WEEK 47

"The Spirit of the Lord is on me, because he has anointed me to preach good news to the poor. He has sent me to proclaim freedom for the prisoners and recovery of sight for the blind, to release the oppressed, to proclaim the year of the Lord's Favor." (LUKE 4:18,19)

WEEK 48

"Every day they continued to meet together in the temple courts. They broke bread in their homes and ate together with glad and sincere hearts, praising God and enjoying the Favor of all the people. And the Lord added to their number daily those who were being saved." (ACTS 2:46,47)

WEEK 49

"Because the patriarchs were jealous of Joseph, they sold him as a slave into Egypt. But God was with him and rescued him from all his troubles. He gave Joseph wisdom and enabled him to gain the Favor of Pharaoh king of Egypt; so he made him ruler over Egypt and all his palace." (ACTS 7:9,10)

WEEK 50

"Having received the tabernacle, our fathers under Joshua brought it with them when they took the land from the nations God drove out before them. It remained in the land until the time of David, who enjoyed God's Favor and asked that he might provide a dwelling place for the God of Jacob." (ACTS 7:45,46)

WEEK 51

"For he says, 'In the time of my favor I heard you, and in the day of salvation I helped you.' I tell you, now is the time of God's Favor, now is the day of salvation." (2 CORINTHIANS 6:2)

WEEK 52

"The Spirit of the Sovereign Lord is on me, because the Lord has anointed me to preach good news to the poor. He has sent me to bind up the brokenhearted, to proclaim freedom for the captives and release for the prisoners, to proclaim the year of the Lord's Favor." (ISAIAH 61:1,2)

Favor Facts

FAVOR IS THE GREATEST HARVEST THAT
YOU COULD EVER RECEIVE FROM GOD.

FAVOR WILL DETERMINE THE
LEVEL OF YOUR INCOME.

FAVOR WILL SHOW UP IN YOUR LIFE WHEN
YOU ASSOCIATE WITH THE RIGHT PEOPLE.

FAVOR WILL CAUSE YOU TO REGAIN
IN ONE DAY WHAT THE ENEMY
HAS STOLEN FOR YEARS.

FAVOR IS A SPENDABLE COMMODITY.
GOD GIVES YOU FAVOR SO THAT YOU
CAN HELP ADVANCE THE KINGDOM.

FAVOR MUST BE A SEED BEFORE
IT BECOMES A HARVEST.

FAVOR WILL BECOME A SHIELD OF
PROTECTION AROUND YOUR LIFE.

FAVOR COMES WHEN YOU CONCENTRATE ON THE SUCCESS OF OTHERS.

FAVOR THAT IS NOT CELEBRATED WILL BECOME FAVOR LOST.

FAVOR WILL INCREASE WHEN YOU PUT OTHERS AHEAD OF YOURSELF.

YOU CAN LOSE FAVOR JUST AS QUICK AS YOU GAINED FAVOR.

FAVOR WILL CAUSE YOUR MEDICAL REPORTS TO CHANGE.

A DAY OF FAVOR WILL CHANGE YOUR LIFE FOREVER.

FAVOR WILL CAUSE YOU TO RISE TO THE TOP IN WHATEVER YOU DO.

FAVOR WILL ACCELERATE YOUR DESTINY.

WHEN YOU DECLARE GOD'S FAVOR WITH
YOUR MOUTH IT WILL INCREASE.

FAVOR IS A REWARD FOR OBEDIENCE.

SPENDING TIME IN PRAYER WITH GOD
WILL INCREASE YOUR FAVOR.

THE CLOSER YOU ARE TO SOMEONE
THE MORE WILLING THEY ARE
TO SHOW YOU FAVOR.

ONE DAY OF FAVOR IS WORTH
A THOUSAND DAYS OF LABOR.

FAVOR WILL INCREASE THE MOMENT
YOU SOLVE A PROBLEM FOR SOMEONE.

EXCELLENCE WILL INCREASE YOUR FAVOR
WITH GOD AND MAN.

WHEN YOU PLANT A SEED OF FAVOR
YOU CAN EXPECT A HARVEST OF FAVOR.

TITHING IS A DOOR TO FINANCIAL FAVOR.

FAVOR WILL ALWAYS
BRING YOU TO THE TOP.

FAVOR IS NOT MERELY AN EVENT,
BUT IT IS A LIFESTYLE.

FAVOR CAN BE LOST AS QUICKLY
AS IT WAS RECEIVED.

THIS YEAR AND EVERY YEAR IS
THE YEAR OF THE LORD'S FAVOR.

FAVOR WILL LEAD YOU WHERE
GOD WANTS TO TAKE YOU.

FAVOR WILL LEAVE YOUR LIFE WHEN YOU
ASSOCIATE WITH WRONG PEOPLE.

FAVOR COULD BE THE
HIDDEN INGREDIENT TO
RESTORATION IN RELATIONSHIPS.

CAN I INTRODUCE YOU TO MY BEST FRIEND?

Before you lay this book aside, make sure you put God first so that you can walk in His Favor, Blessings, and Increase and have the desires of your heart.

First, ask Jesus to cleanse you of your sins. You do not have to clean up your life first—God will do that for you. He will also give you a new heart, new desires, and the Spirit of Truth.

If you truly want a change in your life, then pray this prayer out loud and believe:

> *"Father in Heaven, I've heard Your Word, and I want to be born again. Jesus, cleanse me of my sins. I want to be a child of God. I want to give my life to You. Make me a new person. Be my Lord and Savior.*
>
> *I believe I'm now born again, because the Word of God says I am! Jesus is my Lord. Thank you, Jesus, for a new life. Amen!"*

Now do not go by what you feel. Go by what God's Word says. You are saved—you are born again. Believe it!

WE WANT TO HEAR FROM YOU!

If you prayed this prayer sincerely, call us at 407.770.2020 Also, we want to hear your praise reports and testimonies of God's Favor on your life! Write to us at

DAVE AND CHRISTINE MARTIN
P.O. Box 608150 • Orlando, FL 32860

We want to come into agreement with you!

"If any two of you shall agree it shall be done..."
— Matthew 18:19

PLEASE PRAY FOR GOD'S FAVOR

Dear Dr. Dave and Christine,

Thank you for having your prayer partners join you in prayer for God to show His favor in these areas of my life. I believe that God will provide.

_____

_____

_____

_____

_____

_____

_____

I WANT TO INVEST IN THE MESSAGE OF GOD'S FAVOR

☐ Enclosed is a one time gift of ☐ $111 ☐ $222 ☐ $333 $ _____ 00

Name _____

Address _____

City _____ State _____ Zip _____

Email Address _____ Phone No. _____

I PREFER TO USE MY CREDIT CARD

Check One: ☐ Visa ☐ Mastercard ☐ American Express ☐ Discover

Credit Card Number: _____ Expires: _____

Please record my gift in the amount of $ _____

_____   _____
Authorization Signature   Name as it appears on credit card

dmi
dave martin
INTERNATIONAL

PO BOX 608150 • Orlando, FL 32860
407.770.2020
www.davemartin.org

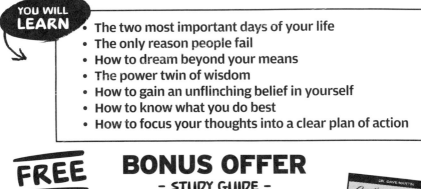

FOCUS | Phenomenal Success Is The Natural Outcome Of A Focused Life

A successful person is the average person, focused. Focus equals power. Focus equals strength and direction. The person who understands and applies the principle of focus to their life becomes a virtually unstoppable force. Focus your life by focusing your thoughts. If you have ever wished to find your focus, it's time you listened to this amazing program.

2 CD's $30

If You Are Going To Be Thinking Anyway... | THINK BIG

An abundant life comes from an abundant mindset. If you want small gradual improvements in your life, work on your behavior. If you want to make quantum progress, work on your thinking. It is the size of your thinking that either propels you forward or holds you back from your ultimate level of achievement. Few people take time to think about their thinking.

2 CD's $30

PASSION

A Passionate Life Has Infinite Horizons

Passion is the fuel that propels the lives of men and women to achievement, excellence and fulfillment in their chosen fields. Passionate people are the source of change in the world. The principle is: Do what you love and what you love will reward you. Finding your passion is the single most important predictor of your future success and fulfillment. You will be remembered for your passion or forgotten for your lack of it.

2 CD's $30

NAME YOUR IT | The Power Of A Seed

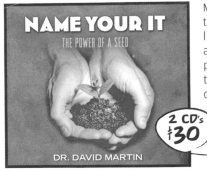

Many people struggle everyday because they do not have enough money. They live lives of frustration, depression, and anguish, never experiencing the joy and peace that has already been provided for them. It is one of the most emotionally charged issues of our lives. People will give up things that are much more valuable than money in order to get more of it. Learn how to receive more... God's way!

2 CD's $30

FAVOR

Favor Will Cause You To Raise To The Top

Favor is the greatest harvest that you will ever receive from God. Favor is better than money. Money cannot buy you Favor, but Favor can bring you money. Favor will show up in your life when you associate with the right people. A day of Favor will change your life forever.

2 CD's $30

THE ULTIMATE RELATIONSHIP

10 Keys For A Life Of Bliss

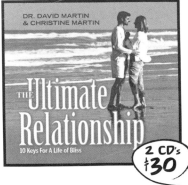

Find simple principles of a really great marriage and the key to unlock the potential in yours. You will laugh, and you will cry as you learn how to have the Ultimate Relationship. You will learn:

- New ways of communicating with each other
- How to recognize your spouse's dominant gifts
- The importance of praying for your spouse
- How to become an instant forgiver

Special Bonus Section for singles

2 CD's $30

NAME YOUR IT

The Power Of A Seed

INTERNATIONAL BEST SELLER

NAME YOUR IT

THE POWER OF A SEED
DR. DAVE MARTIN

$10

Learn how to increase in any area of your life. Understand the power of a Seed. Seed-Faith is sowing something you possess to produce something you have been promised. You can sow a Seed and expect a harvest.

MIRACLES

What To Do When You Need One

$10

You are a miracle, and miracles are happening all around you. The dictionary defines a miracle as a remarkable thing. A miracle is the supernatural intervention of God in the problems of your life. Learn eight powerful keys to receiving your miracle. Unlock the door to many miracles in your future.

EIGHT WAYS TO LIFT YOUR SPIRIT

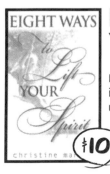

EIGHT WAYS to Lift YOUR Spirit

christine ma

$10

Learn exactly how to lift your own spirit when no one else is around. Your spirits will be lifted as you learn to relax, unwind, and spend time with God. Experience an infusion of energy, and get in touch with the real YOU. You were created to be full of power, purpose, and potential the choices are all up to you.

GOOD MORNING YOUR HIGHNESS

A Daily Guide To Becoming An Ultimate Woman

Good Morning Your Highness!
CR
A Daily Guide To Becoming An Ultimate Woman

$10

RISTINE MARTIN

You will refine you body, mind, and spirit by exploring this unique daily guide for living. Find out that you are 'fearfully and wonderfully made. " (Psalm 139:14). You are a princess in the eyes of God, a Queen in the kingdom, so Queen.... Take your throne and read these lessons there. Enjoy, embrace, and celebrate the uniqueness of who you are.

Visit Us

www.DaveMartin.org

ED YOUNG

"I encourage every pastor to get in touch with Dr. Dave because he will rock your church and take it to a whole *nutha* level in wisdom, success, and finances."

BISHOP HILLIARD

"When Dr. Dave Martin speaks, thousands are affected. He is one of the most prolific and humorous speakers I have ever heard."

JUDAH SMITH

"Dr. Dave will challenge you to look at life different and trust me you will like what you see."

BEN GIBERT

"Dave has an amazing humor that makes learning easy and an ability to motivate those that lack drive, and supercharge the driven to new levels."

BOB HARRISON

"Dave is one of the most powerful and gifted speakers I have ever heard. With skill and humor he drives the points home."

DR. MIKE MURDOCK

"Churches needs his message. Ministers need his wisdom. He will move you to the next level of success."